**DATE DUE**

| | | | |
|---|---|---|---|
| | | | |
| | | | |
| | | | |
| | | | |
| | | | |
| | | | |
| | | | |
| | | | |
| | | | |
| | | | |
| | | | |
| | | | |
| | | | |
| | | | |
| | | | |
| | | | |
| GAYLORD | | | PRINTED IN U.S.A. |

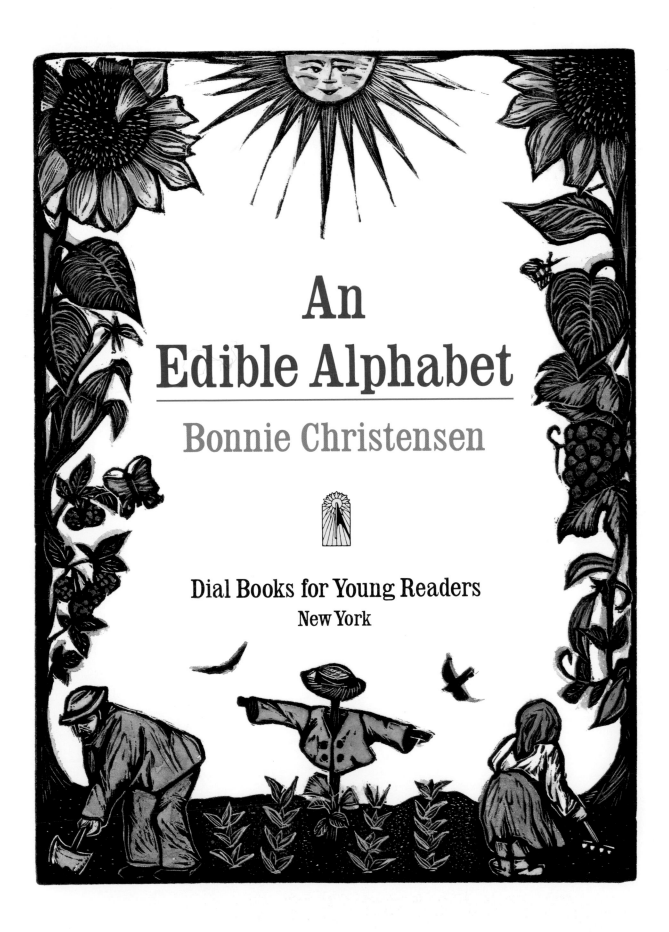

# An
# Edible Alphabet

## Bonnie Christensen

**Dial Books for Young Readers**
New York

For my mother, Theo,
and in memory of my father, Wally

Published by Dial Books for Young Readers
A Division of Penguin Books USA Inc.
375 Hudson Street
New York, New York 10014

Copyright © 1994 by Bonnie Christensen
All rights reserved
Printed in Hong Kong
by South China Printing Company (1988) Limited
Design by Nancy R. Leo
First Edition
1  3  5  7  9  10  8  6  4  2

Library of Congress Cataloging in Publication Data
Christensen, Bonnie.
An edible alphabet / by Bonnie Christensen.—1st ed.
p.  cm.
Summary: Depicts edible plants from Apple to Zucchini
by means of wood engravings. Includes descriptive index.
ISBN 0-8037-1404-1.—ISBN 0-8037-1406-8 (library)
1. Plants, Edible—Juvenile literature.
2. English language—Alphabet—Juvenile literature.
[1. Plants, Edible. 2. Alphabet.] I. Title.
QK98.5.A1C48 1994   581.6′32—dc20   [E]   93-7799   CIP   AC

A Note About the Art and Type

Wood engraving is a form of relief printing in which a sharp,
pointed, metal tool (pictured above) is used to cut an image on the end grain
of a very hard wood. This method was developed in the 1700's to allow for
more detail and less block deterioration than is possible with woodcuts,
which are cut on the softer plank side of the wood. Wood engraving soon became
the most common form of illustration in newspapers, books, and magazines
and was used until the invention of photo etching at the end of the 1800's.

The words and the letters that appear in the art are set in
Clarendon Lightface condensed, a wood type circa 1850 from the collection of the
Ben Lane Printing Shop, Shelburne Museum, Shelburne, Vermont. The woodblocks used for
this book are one hundred and forty years old. Black ink was used for
the woodblock images, and watercolors were then added.

The edible plants pictured are identified by their common or genus names. Other plants of the same genus may not be edible. Just as you should never pick wild mushrooms to eat because some are poisonous, you should never use genus names as a guide for picking wild plants to eat. If you are interested in detailed information, please refer to field guides about edible plants.

# Aa

## Apple

# Bb

# Blueberry

# Cc

# Corn

# Dd

# Dill

# Ee

## Eggplant

# Ff

# Fig

# Gg

**Grape**

# Hh

Hazelnut

# Ii

# Ipomea

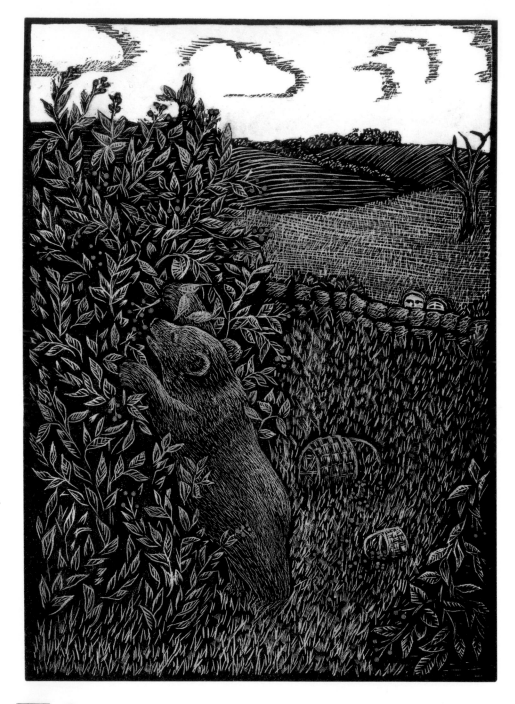

# Jj

# Juneberry

# Kk

## Kale

# Ll

# Lemon

# Mm

**Maple**

# Nn Nasturtium

# Oo

## Oat

# Pp

## Pumpkin

# Qq

Quince

# Rr

## Raspberry

# Ss

# Sunflower

# Tt

Tomato

# Uu

**Ulu**

# V v

## Vanilla

# W w Watermelon

# Xx Xanthorhiza

# Yy

Yam

## Zz

Zucchini

# The Edible Plants

 **Apple** is a round fleshy fruit that grows on trees. Apples are eaten raw, pressed into cider, and used in baking.

 **Blueberry** is a small, sweet, dark-blue berry. Blueberry bushes grow wild and are cultivated. The fruit is used fresh and in baking.

 **Corn** is a grain that grows on a cob covered by a husk. Fresh corn is cooked as a vegetable, while dried corn is eaten as a grain by both people and animals.

 **Dill** is a feathery herb of the parsley family. The flowers, seeds, and leaves are used in cooking and pickling.

 **Eggplant** is a large, purple, oval vegetable of the nightshade family, used for cooking and baking.

 **Fig** is a pear-shaped fruit with a sweet seedy pulp that grows on trees. Figs are used both fresh and dried for eating as a snack and baking.

 **Grape** is a small, juicy berry that grows in clusters on vines. Grapes are eaten fresh, pressed for juice, or dried into raisins.

 **Hazelnut,** or filbert, is the nut of the hazel tree, a member of the birch family. Hazelnuts are eaten plain and used in baking.

 **Ipomea,** or wild potato vine, is a member of the morning glory family. Native Americans named the plant Mecha-Meck and roasted the roots, which resemble the sweet potato, in the ashes of their campfires.

 **Juneberry** is a dark-red berry that grows wild on trees or shrubs in the eastern United States. The berries are eaten fresh, used in baking, or dried.

 **Kale** is a cabbage with loose curly leaves. Its flavor improves in cold weather and it may be harvested well into winter. Kale can be eaten in soup or as a cooked vegetable.

 **Lemon** is a small, yellow citrus fruit that grows on trees in semitropical areas. The lemon's tart juice and rind are used for flavoring.

 **Maple** is a hardwood tree. Each spring it produces a watery sweet sap that is boiled down into maple syrup and sugar.

**Nasturtium** is a garden plant with bright red, yellow, or orange flowers. Both the flower, which has a slightly peppery flavor, and the leaf are used in salads.

 **Oat** is a grain that is ground into flour and rolled into cereal. The grass, on which the grain grows, and the raw oats are used for feeding animals.

 **Pumpkin** is a large orange gourd that grows on a vine. Pumpkins are used in cooking and baking, and are traditionally carved into jack-o'-lanterns on Halloween.

 **Quince** is a hard, round, yellowish fruit that grows on a small tree. The quince is a member of the rose family and is used in making jellies and preserves.

 **Raspberry** is a juicy berry made up of many small drupelets. Raspberries grow on brambly bushes and are eaten raw, used for baking and in jelly or jam.

 **Sunflower** is a tall plant that has a large, yellow, daisylike flower. The center of the flower contains hundreds of sunflower seeds that are eaten by people and birds.

 **Tomato** is a round, juicy, reddish fruit that grows on a vine. Although technically a berry, tomatoes are eaten as vegetables both fresh and cooked.

 **Ulu** is the Hawaiian name for breadfruit; a large, round, green tropical fruit. Breadfruit grows on large trees and tastes like bread when it is baked.

 **Vanilla** is a tropical climbing orchid that bears a podlike bean. The vanilla bean and its extract are used as flavoring in cooking and baking.

 **Watermelon** is a large green melon that grows on a vine. It has a juicy, sweet, pink pulp and many seeds.

 **Xanthorhiza,** or yellow root, is a low shrub that grows wild through the Appalachian Mountains. In folk medicine its root is made into a bitter tea that is used for treating colds and stomach ailments.

 **Yam** is a tuber, or root, of a climbing plant. It is a variety of sweet potato and is used in cooking and baking.

 **Zucchini** is a long, green summer squash that resembles a cucumber. It is eaten fresh as well as in cooking and baking.